My Sloth Wants a Milkshake: Mental Health for Young Humans

Gianna Meloni

AuthorHouse™
1663 Liberty Drive
Bloomington, IN 47403
www.authorhouse.com
Phone: 833-262-8899

Illustrated by Happy Rose

ISBN: 978-1-6655-6638-4 (sc)
ISBN: 978-1-6655-6639-1 (e)

Print information available on the last page.

Published by AuthorHouse 07/26/2022

authorHOUSE®

Note to Grownups

Dear Grownups,

Mental health is important! The conversation about mental health and mental illness does not need to be a scary one and this little book can help get it started. Mental wellness is a part of your young human's life, just the same as physical health. Teaching your young human about reading the signs of their minds and bodies is a lesson best taught early. Thank you for sharing this book with your young humans. I hope this book starts meaningful conversations about mental wellness.

Sincerely,

Gianna Meloni

To my amazing mentor, Katherine V. Warzinski,
who inspires me to reach new heights every day.

Everyone has a sloth. You don't believe me? That's because your sloth is invisible to everyone but you. Your sloth is still there, even if you can't see it!

Do you ever have those days where you don't feel bad but don't feel good—you just feel blah? Perhaps there was a time when you've felt shaky or nervous around other people but don't know why. Other times, you just can't sit still no matter how hard you try. That's your sloth—big, hairy, and a little smelly sometimes— sitting on your back.

Now you're looking at me thinking, "Wow, I have no idea what you are talking about." But we're just getting started here and your sloth is totally dying to get to know you!

Your sloth has been with you since you were born but you might not have noticed it was there. That's because a sloth is very quiet most of the time until you're about the age of 14 (or a little sooner)! It's around this time that your sloth gets to be more talkative. And maybe sometimes you're feeling extra mad or sad because your sloth is trying to get your attention.

Your sloth has a very important job, a job you might not have even heard about. A sloth is another word for your mental health and how you feel each day, whether you're doing GREAT or you're a bit bummy.

"But what is mental health???" you ask. Mental health is your emotions, thoughts, and feelings. Just as you work hard to keep your body healthy, the squishy pink sac in your head needs love too! It's a super hard task to take care of your brain, but I know you'll get the hang of it. You, after all, are a very smart young human if you decided to pick up this book because not a lot of people even *know* about sloths or mental health.

So, what does mental health have to do with sloths?!

Mental health has everything to do with sloths! Just how every person is different, everyone's sloth is different too. Some sloths make you feel very grumpy even on days when the sun is out. Other sloths sit on your back all day and don't let you get anything done.

It is important that you listen to what your sloth has to say, because your feelings happen for a reason. Your sloth might be mad or sleepy or really want a milkshake all at once! The feelings might come out all mixed together and confusing. That's OK. If your sloth wants that milkshake, listen to what your sloth has to say. Think about whether you want that milkshake, or your sloth is using the milkshake to get your attention.

Sometimes the milkshake is hiding how you are really feeling and you might actually be feeling sad or upset.

Now, how you talk to your sloth is very important. Your sloth is your friend, and we always speak to friends in a nice way. Even if your sloth is having a hard day, you should be gentle with yourself and your sloth friend. Find a quiet place for yourself first. Take a breath and try to calm yourself for a moment. You can even close your eyes. Then, try to notice what you are thinking. What are these thoughts saying? Focus on how you are feeling while you are thinking these thoughts. Am I mad? Am I happy? What do I want right now? Your sloth may be quiet at first but once you start to practice this skill, your sloth will speak louder.

Over time, you will learn what your sloth likes and does not like. Be patient and give your sloth lots of love while you learn how to take care of it.

The good news is sloths love to be taken care of and there are plenty of ways to make your sloth happy.

1. Exercise: Your sloth loves a good walk, swim, or bike ride. Moving your body helps produce good feelings in your brain and is great for your sloth.

2. Have a healthy snack: Maybe just what your sloth needs is something to eat or drink. It takes a lot to track how a human feels all the time. The energy you get from your snack will give your sloth the power to take on the day!

3. Talk it out: By keeping all your thoughts and feelings bottled up inside, it can be hard for your sloth to be its best. Talking to a friend or an adult when you're feeling crummy can help your sloth stay happy.

4. Catch some Z's: As you might already know, if you're feeling tired, you might not be at the top of your game. Your sloth can get sleepy too and might make you feel cranky. Taking a short nap or break will help you recharge your sloth when you need to.

5. Do something fun: A happy you means a happy sloth! If you're doing something you like, then you're keeping your sloth in good health and ready for anything.

A super important part of mental health is mental illness. Your brain can feel bad some days just like your body can feel icky. Mental illness can affect how you feel, think, and act. It's very common but you might not even know someone is feeling badly because their sloth is invisible! You can recognize the signs of a sick sloth and help take care of your own. In these next pages, we will learn about some of the mental illnesses that can affect your sloth and how to recognize them.

Anxiety

Everyone has fears or worries. That is completely normal. A sloth with anxiety includes feeling anger, worries, and fears that you cannot control. Let's take a closer look at some signs of anxiety:

- Being very afraid of places where there are people
- Being so scared of something that you can't enjoy things you usually do
- Having worries about things in the future
- Not being able to sleep well
- Being tired, having headaches, or having stomachaches

If you think you feel this way, it is important to talk to an adult to help you with your sick sloth.

Depression

It's OK to have days when you're not feeling like yourself. But if you're not feeling right more often than not, it might be a sign that your sloth might be depressed. Depression is an illness that makes you feel sad, mad, or hopeless. Here are some signs to look out for in your sloth:

- No longer having fun with things you usually like to do
- Eating a lot more or a lot less than usual
- Sleeping a lot or way too much
- Being sleepy or having no energy
- Unable to sit still or focus
- Wanting to harm yourself

If you think you feel this way, it is important to talk to an adult to help you with your sick sloth.

ADHD

ADHD stands for Attention-Deficit/Hyperactivity Disorder. You can see ADHD in your sloth if you have a hard time focusing or sitting still, or you make decisions very fast without thinking about them. Some more signs of ADHD affecting your sloth are:

- Being easily distracted
- Losing or forgetting things a lot
- Having trouble staying seated
- Talking a lot
- Not feeling very good about yourself
- Having a hard time waiting your turn

If you think you feel or act this way, it is important to talk to an adult to help you with your sick sloth.

Eating Disorders

How you feel about your body and about food can also come from your sloth. It sounds scary, but an Eating Disorder just means you spend a lot of time thinking about what your body looks like and wanting to lose weight. Other signs of an Eating Disorder include:

- Exercising way too much to lose weight
- Not letting yourself eat or starving yourself
- Eating way too much
- Hiding food for yourself
- Being in a not good mood a lot of the time

If you think you feel or act this way, it is important to talk to an adult to help you with your sick sloth.

Signs of Mental Illness

It is possible to notice that you're just not doing well but you might not know what is going on with your sloth. Here are some signs of odd sloth behavior that might point to a mental illness:

- Feeling sad all the time
- Not wanting to see anyone
- Thinking a lot about not wanting to be here anymore
- Feeling mad a lot
- Gaining or losing weight
- Not being able to sleep
- Not being able to focus
- Having stomachaches or headaches a lot

So now that you are officially an awesome sloth expert, let's go over some of the fun stuff we learned.

1. It is super important to check in with your sloth each day to see how you're feeling. Don't ignore your sloth! If you're not feeling right, try one of the five cool activities we went over earlier.
2. Try your best. It's not easy to learn a new skill but the more you practice the sooner you'll become a sloth pro.

3. Mental illness doesn't have to be scary. It is just another part of life! If you take care of your sloth and listen to what it has to say, you will be in great shape!
4. When in doubt, reach out to an adult for help with your sloth. Emotions, feelings, and thoughts can get pretty messy, so it is helpful to have someone older to talk to.

Remember: every sloth is different and amazing in their own way. Spend time learning about your sloth and how to love them.

Don't forget to give your sloth a milkshake every once in a while to let them know they're doing a great job. Sloths love a good milkshake.

Resources:

Centers for Disease Control and Prevention. (2022, April 19). *Anxiety and depression in children.* Centers for Disease Control and Prevention. Retrieved July 17, 2022, from https://www.cdc.gov/childrensmentalhealth/depression.html

Mayo Clinic Staff. (2019, June 25). *Attention-deficit/hyperactivity disorder (ADHD) in children.* Mayo Clinic. Retrieved July 17, 2022, from https://www.mayoclinic.org/diseases-conditions/adhd/symptoms-causes/syc-20350889

Mayo Clinic Staff. (2022, March 2). *Mental illness in children: Know the signs.* Mayo Clinic. Retrieved July 17, 2022, from https://www.mayoclinic.org/healthy-lifestyle/childrens-health/in-depth/mental-illness-in-children/art-20046577

Ocklenburg, S. (2021, June 18). *At what age does mental illness begin?* Psychology Today. Retrieved July 17, 2022, from https://www.psychologytoday.com/us/blog/the-asymmetric-brain/202106/what-age-does-mental-illness-begin

Parekh, R., M.D., M.P.H (Ed.). (2018). *What is mental illness?* Psychiatry.org - What is Mental Illness? Retrieved July 17, 2022, from https://psychiatry.org/patients-families/what-is-mental-illness

Smith , K., PhD, LPC (2021, September 10). *Eating Disorders in Children 12 and Under: Learn the Warning Signs.* PSYCOM. Retrieved July 17, 2022, from https://www.psycom.net/eating-disorders-in-children

What is mental health? What Is Mental Health? | MentalHealth.gov. (2022, February 28). Retrieved July 17, 2022, from https://www.mentalhealth.gov/basics/what-is-mental-health

About the Author

Gianna Meloni grew up in Washington, DC, and currently resides in Boston, Massachusetts. She is a graduate of Yale University and a former Division I college ice hockey goalie. At Yale, she double majored in Psychology and English and is currently attending Boston College to become a Psychiatric Mental Health Nurse Practitioner. Her passions include changing the culture of mental health and society's perception of mental illness. Gianna is interested in serving young adults from the ages of 8 to 25 and educating people of all ages on the importance of mental wellness.

Printed in the United States
by Baker & Taylor Publisher Services